FOOTPRINTS ON THE MOON

ALSO BY SETH GODIN

What to Do When It's Your Turn (and It's Always Your Turn)

Poke the Box

We Are All Weird

Linchpin

Whatcha Gonna Do With That Duck?

The Icarus Deception

This Might Work

All Marketers are Liars

Tribes

Small Is the New Big

Meatball Sundae

The Dip

Free Prize Inside

Purple Cow

Survival Is Not Enough

The Big Red Fez

Unleashing the Ideavirus

Permission Marketing

FIND THEM ALL AT SETHGODIN.COM

FOOTPRINTS ON THE MOON

What Changemakers Know

SETH GODIN

The Domino Project
Published by Do You Zoom, Inc.

Exterior cover images from NASA archives
Interior cover image by Thom Schneider on Unsplash©

The setting was right out of a movie.

There was a roaring campfire. It was a cold October night and I was lucky enough to be sitting with family and friends and colleagues.

Standing next to the campfire, the subject of our rapt attention, was Neil Armstrong. As he told us the story of the Apollo mission, a full moon began to rise in the cloudless sky.

Casually, as he looked over his shoulder at the moon behind him, he said, "I've been there."

That sets the bar pretty high.

PART ONE

Make change happen.

You are in charge.

Three things changemakers know

1. Committed, creative people can change the world (in fact, they're the only ones who do). You can do it right now, and you can make more change than you can possibly imagine.

2. You cannot change everyone. Instead, asking "Who's it for?" can focus your actions and help you deal with the non-believers (in your head and in the outside world).

3. Building with intent is never aimless. Everything you do matters, and there's no time to waste your efforts. "What's it for?" is the posture of an effective agent of change.

One answer and two questions

You. As in, "You can do it." You're the one and the time is now.

Who? As in, "Who's it for?" Because it can't be for everyone.

What? As in, "What's it for?" Every step matters.

Change

That's what we do.

That's what we make.

We change things.

We build bridges, get policies approved and teach others how to do it too.

We work to ease suffering, to shine a light, to make things better.

That project you're working on—it will lead to a new hospital, or a better way to serve your customers, or a system to protect an ecosystem. You might be working to make a bigger profit, hire more people or teach someone to do better.

This work moves us from here to where we need to go.

Every time we change something for the better, we're doing our best work. And we know we could do it even better.

Teams and individuals are two sides of our reality

Nothing important happens unless others pitch in. Our distributed model of teamwork now makes it possible to build something bigger than yourself, far faster, and with more impact, than ever before.

But this teamwork can't happen without leadership. And no one is capable of leading the work you care about better than you are.

The power to make change happen

It's easy to see what needs changing. There are processes and places and people that need to work differently.

Our ability to make things more fair or more efficient has never been greater. The internet amplifies our voice when we speak up, and the tools of the net give us the leverage to do more than we ever had any right to expect.

This shift to making change has taken many people by surprise.

Just do your job

In the old model, the original model of industrial work, your job was to do your job. Making change was someone else's work.

It's impossible to overstate how essential this mantra was to just about every large organization. "It's not your job to ask why, it's your job to do precisely what I said."

The company did the thinking, and you did the work.

The problem with that approach is that companies aren't nearly as good at thinking as people are. And that during times of change, we need the people near the problem to be working hard at solving it.

Recently, leaders began to realize that "Think for yourself" was incompatible with "Think what I tell you to think."

It turns out that giving up the care and insight of everyone in the organization was too high a price to pay for the efficiency of compliance.

You're not the boss, but you are in charge

In charge of how you spend your time.

In charge of the questions you ask.

In charge of the insight that you produce.

In the powerful, horizontal organization, each of us decides what to learn next, who to talk with next, what to move up on the agenda.

Show me your to-do list and you've told me a lot about your choices.

"Here, I made this."

"I," as in me, you, us, the person who's on the line. This is the work of a human. The audience can make a direct connection between you and the thing you're offering.

"Made," because it took effort, originality and skill.

"This" is not a wishy-washy concept. It's concrete and finite. It didn't used to exist, and now it does.

And, "here," because the idea is a gift, a connection transferred from person to person.

These four words carry generosity, intent, risk and intimacy.

The more we say them, and mean them, and deliver on them, the more art and connection we create.

And we create change for a living.

Changemakers in charge

It's pretty simple, this new reality:

You're here to make change.

Time is fleeting and you only get today once.

Now that you're in charge, there are three simple ways you can make that change with more focus, energy and success.

First, you can embrace the fact that you are able to get unstuck.

Second, you can focus on the few, not everyone.

And third, you can bring intention to your work, making every step along the way count.

You may not be going to the moon, but wherever you're headed, it's important.

"I don't believe in art, but I believe in artists..."

MARCEL DUCHAMP

PART TWO

YOU.

There's no such thing as writer's block.

I know why you're stuck and I think I can help

Thanks for caring so much. It's your care that makes everything worthwhile. Your caring creates our culture. It contributes to meaning. It matters.

But the reason you're stuck is that you care so much. When you care this much, it's easy to get stuck.

It has nothing to do with talent. Nothing to do with inherent gifts. Nothing to do with your horoscope…

No, the reason that you're stuck is that you care. You care about the work, about your reputation, about the critics, about what happens to your work.

I don't want you to care less; I'd like you to care even more.

And to ship your very best work.

You can. Here we go.

The chance of a lifetime

The world is changing.

The stakes are high.

You have more leverage than ever before, and possibly more leverage than you will ever have again.

You can reach more people, change more minds, enable more connection and possibility than ever before.

Let's not waste it because we're afraid.

Magical powers

Humans are the only creatures we know of who are capable of making change happen. Of course, beavers can build dams and bees can build hives, but humans are actually capable of changing the culture.

We do things that have never been done before.

We create connections that eliminate loneliness and produce productivity.

We shine a light in a dark place.

Most of all, we can change standards and expectations. Our work in changing our own culture is so mysterious and powerful that we are apparently causing magic to happen.

And yet, just when we need it most, it often seems that our wand is out of juice, that our ability to speak or write or invent or connect deserts us.

Where did it go?

It was there just a heartbeat ago.

When you were younger, you had something interesting to say, a funny idea, a vision of how things might be different.

It doesn't seem that long ago when you were one of the finest finger painters in the class. You could put together a poem or a clever idea without a sweat.

And now, it seems like it might be gone. That you're blocked.

We talk about aiming high, we know that there are footprints on the moon, we see others living in a zone of possibility. But too often, we feel stuck with what we have instead of being motivated to bring the change that's possible. Your creativity is blocked.

Not just the ability to write a novel, but the insight and desire to say something important at the weekly staff meeting. The inspiration and flow necessary to write a new business plan, figure out the chords for a new song or solve a particularly difficult problem in your research.

It just won't come. You're empty. You have writer's block.

This is painful. The painful zone between "I have something to contribute," and "I can't figure out what to say or do."

Some people live in this zone for years.

It hurts.

It sucks the life out of you and everyone around you.

Writer's block is a curse. Except...

There's no such thing as writer's block

There's no plumber's block or bookkeeper's block or driver's block. People don't wake up in the morning unable to speak, suffering from some sort of talker's block either.

How is it that this affliction, the inability to come up with original ideas, to figure out new solutions, to sing and paint and inspire and invent—how is it that this happens *to* us?

People get warts. They get glaucoma. Sometimes, tragically, they get cancer. But I don't believe you can get writer's block.

To be clear, I don't deny that you're feeling stuck.

But writer's block is a myth, a protective cocoon, not an ailment. You talked yourself into it and you can work yourself out of it.

Does knowing it help us?

For most of us, the reality of writer's block was never really in doubt. We've felt the subtle avoidance instinct, or experienced the white flash of terror. We've stared at keyboards waiting for the blank screen to fill itself, and we've stood on podiums, hands clammy, with nothing particularly important to say.

It's hard to hear that writer's block is a myth.

Because, of course, if it's real to you, knowing it's a myth doesn't help very much.

Except it does.

When I was a kid, I was sure there was a monster under my bed. My dad let me know that of course, monsters weren't real.

Didn't matter; the monster didn't go away.

Not immediately, anyway.

But it's funny, because as I think back to it, the monster did begin to fade shortly thereafter.

Real things don't fade away. Real things don't come in and out of focus. That's what ghosts and myths do.

By acknowledging that writer's block is a cultural mirage, we establish a foundation for working with it and ultimately eliminating it.

Writer's block is a painful suit of armor

It's armor we chose. Armor against the outside world, against criticism, against failure.

It's a nearly perfect protection.

Except that it hurts.

Blame it on Shelley

Mary Shelley invented Frankenstein. An entire genre of writing and movies. The seeds of science fiction. Mary Shelley was a giant.

Her husband? Not so much.

Percy Bysshe Shelley started the writer's block meme. One of the great Romantic poets, he wrote:

> Poetry is not like reasoning, a power to be exerted according to the determination of the will. A man cannot say, "I will compose poetry." The greatest poet even cannot say it; for the mind in creation is as a fading coal, which some invisible influence, like an inconstant wind, awakens to transitory brightness; this power arises from within, like the color of a flower which fades and changes as it is developed, and the conscious portions of our natures are unprophetic either of its approach or its departure.

A fading coal? Sheesh. I'd much rather read his wife Mary's stuff. At least Frankenstein knew what was up.

As Joan Acocella has pointed out, before Shelley, writing was up to us. It was work, and it was work that we could choose to do, when we needed or wanted to do it. After his rant, the poets, then the novelists, then the screenwriters and then the ad copywriters gradually adopted the unproductive and tortured narrative of the muse.

And now, in a modern world where everyone can speak up, where anyone can contribute, where anyone can share an invention, all of us are threatened with writer's block.

I just don't feel like it.

I'm not inspired.

I don't see it.

It's not coming.

I'm stuck.

In their version of the world, you can be blocked because creativity is a wind, and if your sails aren't in just the right location, you will sit at sea, becalmed, stranded, just waiting for scurvy to consume you in a slow, agonizing, painful death.

Learning to see

Once you can see the fraud of an ailment that we call writer's block, you'll be able to dance past it.

It's elusive, mysterious and wily, but once you see it, you're on your way.

Closing the craft gap

It took Miles Davis about 72 hours to write and record his greatest album, *Kind of Blue*. In less time than it takes most people to clean their garage, he changed jazz.

It's no surprise that stories like this lead us to believe that creativity only comes in gusts, and that it happens to other people, to geniuses.

Here's the thing: Miles made 48 studio albums. Not many of them changed jazz forever. Miles performed in concert hundreds of times. Few of them were titanic acts of creative genius.

Bob Dylan has recorded even more albums than Miles did. And given more concerts.

Ella Fitzgerald left both these guys in the dust. She recorded more than 200 albums and sold 40,000,000 copies of her work.

The thing is, these artists are plumbers.

They show up, they do their work. They learn a craft and they practice it. And every once in a while, they record *Kind of Blue*.

If you need your appendix out, you don't want an inspired surgeon. You want a trained pro who has removed 300 appendixes. There's a craft to it, and the presumption is that practice, particularly rigorous practice, leads to better outcomes.

While we've built a cult of fascination about the first-time novelist, most of the time that's merely a misnomer. While you might be celebrating someone's first *published* novel, it's certainly not the first thing she wrote.

We are craftspeople. Not sailors, dependent on fickle winds. But craftspeople, able to do the hard work of making a difference.

If I'm a genius...

Then you're a genius. The geniuses, the others, the ones who have what we don't, they're everywhere, with more of them showing up daily. Einstein and Novogratz and Mother Teresa. Orators. Programmers. Painters. Writers. Leaders. Comedians...

If they're geniuses, so are you.

Genius is an act, something we do. It's not a person.

A combination of poor dancing and bad habits

So, if writer's block isn't an organic disruption of our ability to catch the winds from the muse, what is it?

It's a pretty simple combination of two things: We don't dance well with fear. And we create habits that make it unlikely we ever will.

We can become creative again gradually, the same way we got into this box. We can become creative by seeing fear differently and by following the most important practice of the craftsperson: good habits.

Buzzer management

I started the quiz team at my high school. Alas, I didn't do so well at the tryouts, so I ended up as the coach, but we still made it to the finals.

It took me 30 years to figure out the secret of getting in ahead of the others who also knew the answer (because the right answer is no good if someone else gets the buzz):

You need to press the buzzer before you know the answer.

As soon as you realize that you might be able to identify the answer by the time you're asked, buzz.

Between the time you buzz and the time you're supposed to speak, the answer will come to you. And if it doesn't, the penalty for being wrong is small compared to the opportunity to get it right.

This feels wrong in so many ways. It feels reckless, careless and selfish. Of course we're supposed to wait until we're sure before we buzz. But the waiting leads to a pattern of not buzzing.

No musician is sure her album is going to be a hit. No entrepreneur is certain that every hire is going to be a good one. No parent can know that every decision they make is going to be correct.

What separates this approach from mere recklessness is the experience of discovering (in the right situation) that buzzing makes your work better, that buzzing helps you dig deeper, that buzzing inspires you.

The habit is simple: Buzz first; buzz when you're confident that you've got a shot. Buzz, buzz, buzz. If it gets out of hand, we'll let you know.

The act of buzzing leads to leaping, and leaping leads to great work.

Not the other way around.

Looking into the eye of the sun

I'm well aware of the risk of writing about writer's block. I feel it looming, with every sentence I write. Like a black cloud that keeps getting darker as I get closer to it, writer's block isn't happy that I'm writing about it.

I find 20 ways to stop, 15 ways to stall, 10 ways to insert fluff.

The closer I get, the harder it fights with me…

And then I remember that there are footprints on the moon.

This moment, the one we have right now, is the chance of a lifetime. I'm not interested in wasting it. Are you?

The brittleness

Some of the most successful creators I know are very difficult to be around.

They're holding on for dear life. They're afraid to talk about their work, their process and most of all, their dreams and fears.

As if examining their genius will make it go away.

And yet…

Some of the most successful creators I know are happy to talk about their craft. They lay ideas the way some people lay bricks. They understand it's not about magic, it's about intent and purpose and process.

All part of the mythology of writer's block. Looking at your genius doesn't make it disappear (unless you think it will).

On dancing with our fear

At some point in reading this book, most people are expecting that the sails will puff up, the muse's winds will return and they will magically, and blessedly, find themselves unstuck.

We desire to be freed of the fear and to get back on track (doing our regular art). But that won't happen.

Your fond dream won't happen because the fear won't go away. It can't go away. It's not going to go away.

Perhaps you didn't have fear years ago, when you were younger. You had a lot less to lose. You were more desperate. You were distracted by hormones and new experiences and the endless excitement of novelty.

But now, now you have fear. Steve Pressfield's Resistance. The fear of being caught out as the fraud that you know you are. The fear of losing it all. The fear of having to begin again.

No one wants to be laughed at by their peers. Most of all, not you, right here, right now.

That fear is evolutionarily reasonable; there are good reasons for it.

That fear is reinforced by our families, by our culture, by our economic system.

You don't get rewarded for blowing it, you get rewarded for doing it well. Again.

Fear, then, is built in—a protective sheath designed to keep us from various forms of failure.

Our narrative about fear, though, has gotten out of control. We take a simple neurochemical process and build up strata of stories around it. Vivid, detailed visions of failure, experienced in advance. Complex analyses of what we think others are thinking, what we believe the boss or the critic or the audience wants.

We seek to reverse-engineer each of these narratives, working hard to find firm ground, a patch of dry land we can stand on and get back to work.

But these narratives are perfectly constructed so that we'll never quite make it.

That's on purpose, of course. If we could find dry land to be creative upon, the narrative would have failed us, the muse that seeks to hide and find safety away from the danger of creativity.

No, the fear can never go away.

But we can learn to dance with it.

We can use it as a compass.

We can replace "but" with "and."

The "and" replacement

In *The Art of Possibility*, Ben and Roz Zander teach us a super-simple word replacement trick.

"I want to write a new article, but I'm afraid," becomes:

"I want to write a new article, and I'm afraid."

A simple statement of fact. The collision of two situations, apparently (if you believe the "but") in contradiction to each other, but in fact, totally compatible.

Let's start with an easier one, concocted by Roz:

"I'm on vacation but it's raining."

The rain could ruin your vacation, particularly if you're at a ski resort, where rain appears to be a deal killer.

But, the replacement of "but" with "and" means that you've just opened the door to a hundred options.

"I'm on vacation at a ski resort and it's raining."

"I'm on vacation at a ski resort and it's raining, which means I finally have time to make the 28-ingredient molé that I've always wanted to spend the day on."

When you think about your creative block, substituting the "and" means that you've finally acknowledged the first step: I'm afraid and I need to dance with that.

Reassurance is futile

Of course, being told that everything will be okay is a nice thing to hear. It can build our confidence and soothe our fears.

But… Everything isn't going to be okay. You will be rejected. You will have lousy ideas. You will feel stuck. Not only that, but people will resist the change you bring to them, they will be unappreciative, friends will doubt your sanity or your sincerity.

Which might bring you back looking for more reassurance.

But it will never be enough.

It can never be enough.

Reassurance doesn't scale.

And reassurance plays into the mythos of writer's block, because it implies that you need an external life preserver to actually do your work.

Don't seek reassurance. When you accept that you and you alone are going to produce your work of genius, you have the set the proper hook.

You're on the hook to make change happen. And telling you it will all be alright doesn't help.

Simply do the work.

"But I don't know the right answer."

That's the only honest thing you can say.

No one knows the right answer, not if the work is interesting.

If we wait until we know the right answer before we speak up, we will never speak up, because the only way to move forward is to explore. Acknowledging that it's not our job to be perfect is the first step on the road to being interesting.

Mise en place is its own reward

Large and impressive, the New Caledonian crow makes a hook out of twigs to catch prey. Tool use is something that defines a professional: Without our tools, we're quickly going to rank behind the crows on the hierarchy of achievement.

Chefs defined the idea of *mise en place*: Organizing every ingredient and sauce, pre-cut, pre-measured and ready to go before the rush. In many commercial kitchens, this is the job of a junior staffer, a way to earn her stripes on the path to running the place.

The act of creating this palette of tools is its own reward. It reminds us of what we're here to do. It belies Shelley's foolish notion of the muse. With the presence of our tools, our systems, our workplace, we have established that we are here to work. To dance.

Fetishizing the tool preparation is just as bad as not doing it at all. The tools are never the result, they are only a method to achieve it.

The Rosenzweig Technique*

Get a stack of blank postcards, the kind with a stamp already on them. Address each of them to yourself, probably at home.

The challenge is simple: Four times a day, fill a postcard with an idea, a message to yourself from today to tomorrow. And then mail it.

A few days later, handwritten ideas from your past yourself will begin to arrive.

Each day, when you get home from work, you'll get three or four (or even five) ideas worth reading.

As each arrives, your job is to take that germ and write it up, expand it, put it into the word processor on your computer.

**Named for Franz Rosenzweig, an author who served in the first World War. He wrote his ideas on postcards and sent them to his mom for safekeeping. He turned them into a book years later.*

It's the end of the day, so there's no need to worry about checking your email.

Do this for five weeks, for 35 days, for 140 cards. Do it without cease, without hesitation, without regard for whether it's perfect or not.

When we remove the excuses we allow the fear to shine through

It seems as though we ought to do the opposite, to bury the fear and hope that, without light, it will fade away. So we go knife shopping. So we organize our tools. So we wait for the right emotional moment to get in touch with our muse, all in an effort to distract ourselves from the fear that is causing us so much pain.

Of course it's painful to be afraid.

That's the job of fear. It keeps us alive by providing enough pain to talk us out of doing stupid, dangerous things.

But there's a difference between pain and suffering.

As Pema Chödrön tells us, suffering is what happens when we insist that pain isn't fair, that it must leave us alone, that we can will the pain away.

All that remote controlling is called suffering.

But what if we realize that pain is part of the deal, the flipside of tails for a life that sometimes includes heads?

"I'm afraid," is a fine way to start.

"I'm afraid and I'm going to create now," is an even better next step.

"I'm afraid and I'm going to ship this now."

Limiting decisions

Once we accept that writer's block is a myth, we can more easily see all the ways we fuel that myth. Waiting for inspiration is just one of them, but a great place to begin.

Successful, productive professionals often do their work on schedule. They outline when they're supposed to outline, write when they are supposed to write. They learn new skills, open themselves up to outside ideas, go on promotional tour—all on schedule.

They don't spend any time at all making decisions about what task to do next. Instead, they spend all their creative energy on the work itself.

How can you possibly do this work on schedule if you're waiting for inspiration?

Well, it turns out that being on a schedule is a fabulous way to become inspired.

Simply do it—not "just do it"

Nike did creators a disservice by popularizing the slogan "Just do it." It's easy to read the word "just" as a throwaway. "Just get it over with." Or, "Whatever, just throw it out there."

This is another of the 84 ways that we sacrifice our work to our fear.

It's far more productive to merely do it. As in "only," without distraction.

Simply do that work.

Simply show up.

Simply create.

Simply ship the work.

Without commentary or drama or a manufactured crisis.

Merely do it.

If it makes you feel more important, you can say, "Only do it."

Your work is important. Important enough to do. Important enough to focus on. And mostly, important enough to ship without excuses.

84 ways we sacrifice our work to our fear

1. Stall
2. Expand the project so it cannot move forward
3. Shrink the project so that it doesn't matter
4. Ship crap
5. Don't ship work that can be improved by others
6. Refuse to listen to generous critics
7. Eagerly listen to well-meaning but chicken-hearted critics

8. Sacrifice the work for the commercial short-term
9. Hide from deadlines
10. Become a diva
11. Compromise on the good parts
12. Compromise on the hard parts
13. Assume that inspiration lies in a bottle or a pill
14. Don't go to work
15. Work all the time
16. Wait for the muse
17. Talk about the work too early, looking for a reason to abandon it
18. Don't talk about the work with the right people, crippling it
19. Define the work as you and you as the work, making it all personal
20. Work only when inspiration strikes
21. Fall behind on domain knowledge
22. Copy everything
23. Copy nothing
24. Feed the fires of jealousy
25. Taunt yourself
26. Announce that the important work takes longer
27. Expect applause
28. Demand cash commensurate with effort or insight and hold back until it arrives

29. Avoid sales calls
30. Read your reviews
31. Memorize your reviews
32. Respond to your reviews
33. Catastrophize
34. Focus on your impending or eventual death
35. Assume immortality as a way of stalling
36. Listen to people who are afraid
37. Confuse perfectionism with quality
38. Hold on tighter as the ship date approaches
39. Let go too soon as the ship date approaches
40. Miss ship dates on a regular basis
41. Don't set ship dates
42. Redefine your zone of contribution to be smaller than it needs to be, thus letting yourself off the hook
43. Surround yourself with people who have small dreams
44. Polish your excuses
45. Whine about writer's block

46 through 84...Insert your own well-polished forms of suffering right here.

Confusion about running errands

Errands are not a form of *mise en place*. They need to be done (you need groceries and a driver's license), but they're not tools.

If you're running errands instead of creating, you're stalling, you're hiding.

(And yes, we run errands when we spend a day answering email, or a day in meetings, or a day taking notes and pretending to pay attention in class.)

Domain knowledge: "To Serve Man"

It's entirely possible you're not familiar with that classic episode of *The Twilight Zone*. You might not know who Lefsetz or LeGuin or Laplace are either. But, if you're hoping to create important work, domain knowledge is at the heart of your craft.

I was talking to someone dedicating his career to working in newspapers. I asked him what he thought of the work of Jeff Jarvis. He had no idea what I was talking about.

I met a musician the other day, and asked her how her work without a label was going. I referenced something by Bob Lefsetz. She didn't know who I meant.

The last time I was at an event for librarians, I mentioned Maria Popova. Blank stares.

A podcaster asked me a question, and I wondered if he admired the path Krista Tippett had taken. He had no clue.

A colleague was explaining his work in memetics to me. I asked about Dawkins and Blackmore. You guessed it...

Or Kenji on food, Cader on publishing, Underhill on retail, Lewis on direct mail copywriting and on and on...

We would never consent to surgery from a surgeon who hadn't been to medical school, and perhaps even more important, from someone who hadn't kept up on the latest medical journals and training. And yet there are people who take pride in doing their profession from a place of naïveté, unaware of or unfamiliar with the most important voices in their field.

The line between an amateur and professional keeps blurring, but for me, the posture of understanding both the pioneers and the state of the art is essential. An economist doesn't have to agree with Keynes, but she better know who he is.

If you don't know who the must-reads in your field are, find out before your customers and competitors do.

Too much doing, not enough knowing

Brian Koppelman, the renowned screenwriter and showrunner, has seen more movies than you have. He may have seen more movies than anyone I've ever met. And that's not merely a sign of passion. His understanding of what's come before gives him the platform and the standing to help figure out what's going to come next.

Growing up, I read every single book in the science fiction section of the Clearfield Public Library. From Asimov to Zelazny, all of them. Ten years later, when I launched a line of science fiction computer games, the domain knowledge opened the door to understanding what might work.

The point is not to copy, but in fact, to avoid copying. Our best commercial work reminds people of what they've seen before.

Creativity doesn't repeat itself, but it rhymes.

Motivation is the word for what allows us to dance with our fear

I don't blog every day because I have a good idea.

I have a good idea because I blog every day.

The danger of wifi—you react to the initiation of others, squandering your own

It's a modern malady: Invisible wifi radiation rays are sapping our energy, giving us mysterious diseases and generally messing with our biome.

Of course, wifi doesn't do anything at all to our bodies.

But the wifi that's connected to your device is probably destroying your work.

As soon as you wake up, you are a pawn in someone else's game. Your connection to the internet puts you into a position where you need to react or respond to someone else's initiative. You are socially expected to answer their email, like their posts, or continue an argument long after that argument stopped being interesting to you.

In the days of the telephone, smart creators figured out when they'd check their messages, only calling folks back when it suited their productivity schedule. Today, though, the Pavlovian rewards of clearing an inbox or seeing what others are saying is so strong, it's difficult to resist.

Search engines and online databases are a Trojan Horse for the emotion (and time) sucks of email and social media. While we can save hours finding the right answer (Ella made 200 albums?!), we can also find ourselves yak shaving for hours.

The solution is draconian and obvious: Turn it off.

Not all the time. Perhaps 10 daylight hours of wifi is enough. That still leaves you six hours to actually get some work done.

Selling is where the juice lies

Is there any profession that more people seek to avoid? Even salespeople work hard to avoid making sales calls. It's hard to imagine a bookkeeper who spends his day not keeping books, or a doctor who actively avoids seeing patients.

But sales…

It's not surprising that true sales (as opposed to order-taking, which is a different thing entirely) is anathema to many people. Sales is about change (turning "I never heard of it" into "no" and then "yes"). Sales is about upending the status quo of what the world was like before you got there. Most of all, sales is about intentionally creating tension, the tension of "Maybe," the tension of "This might not work," the tension of "What will I tell my boss…"

Why would anyone sign up for that?

But this tension is precisely the tension that we dance with as creators.

This is how we get sold on the thing we're creating before we share it. We must sell ourselves first, before we can sell anyone else.

But learning to sell other people is the single best way to learn to sell yourself.

The juiciness lies in the objections, in seeing the gears turn, in hearing someone persuade themselves that they love what's on offer.

Ultimately, a successful sales call results in enrollment.

Enrollment

Enrollment is the acknowledgment that we are on a journey together.

The Tin Man enrolls with Dorothy to go to see the Wizard. He has his own agenda. He's after his own reward, as are the Scarecrow and the Lion.

But even though each member of the troupe has their own goal in mind, they are all enrolled in the same journey, with the same agreed-upon roles and rules and, probably, timeframes.

Once people are enrolled, you can get down to it.

Before that, you're spending all your time getting butts in seats, reassuring the masses, primping up the benefits of your offer.

After enrollment, though, the shift goes from "you" to "we." WE are off to see the Wizard. WE are engaged in this process, this journey, this performance.

To the enrolled, all we need to do is point. We can gesture over there and the team will follow. They know what it's for.

To the un-enrolled, though, all we can say is, "Sorry, it's not for you."

It's not for you

Waiting for Godot might be my favorite play. Beckett was the Marcel Duchamp of theatre, and this play is a masterpiece. Most people hate it.

They hate it because it's not where they want to go for two hours in a theatre. They hate it because it's not the journey they signed up for. They hate it because it doesn't actually remind them of the kind of plays they like.

What does this remind you of?

Adoption of your idea is driven by culture. People like us do things like this.

And of course, we can't understand all of your idea until we embrace it, so we're stuck—afraid to embrace something we don't understand, and unable to understand it until we embrace it.

Culture solves this problem by seeking genres, analogies, things that rhyme.

Creative work is never the duplicate of something that came before. But it usually reminds us of something that came before. It fits into the taxonomy of the genre.

Generic is a bad thing. The fresh voice in a genre, the one that breaks just the right rules—that's a good thing.

The search for certainty is at the heart of our block

In an industrial world, the high-stakes marketplace requires us to be right. Every time.

Make a mistake on the assembly line and you lose your job.

Make an error at the bank and you're out.

But the world we seek to create doesn't exist yet, and it has no right answers. If we knew how to do this work, we would have done it already.

Certainty, then, must be elusive, because we can't know for sure. The elusiveness isn't a problem, it's not a bug, it's not something to be eliminated. The uncertainty is the point.

The real lesson of improv only begins with "yes, and"

Improv done right is thrilling. It's leaping without a net, an uncalculated freefall in which two or more people dance as the clock ticks and the fear rises. Will they connect?

The improv team (and it only works as a team, players in an infinite game) tosses the ball back and forth, raising the stakes as they weave something out of nothing.

The first rule of improv is that "no" is a deal killer. When the ball comes to you, the answer is always, "yes, and..." Forward motion is the only sort of motion that we're interested in.

When ego shows up, the ball slows down, and "no" appears at the same time that possibility fades away.

"Yes, and" is a tactic, and a good one. But it's insufficient.

The real lesson is the power of uncertainty and the acknowledgment of the absurdity of writer's block. Of course there's no writer's block in improv. All there is is ego, seeking control. All there is is fear, putting up walls. When we let the ego subside and acknowledge the fear, then we're able to say, "yes, and."

Saturday Night Live doesn't go on at 11:30 because it's ready. It goes on because it's 11:30.

Anchor up.

Anchor up

We like to keep promises. It's hard to be a successful, happy person if you don't.

We hesitate to make a promise like, "The show will be on at 11:30," because we're not sure we can make it happen.

The subconscious is powerful indeed. If it knows that we've made a promise, that the book is due, that the brainstorming session is starting, that the pitch is due at the VC—it will work overtime to help us keep that promise.

Anchors can drag us down. That's their job on a boat.

But for a creative person, an anchor can also be a beacon, the thing we work toward, relentlessly.

Not because it's perfect.

But because it's 11:30.

We promised.

What to say to a generous critic

"Thank you."

That critic just gave you a clue.

She told you what might work. Not for the market, probably, but for her and for people like her.

And if she's any good, she delivered that criticism without indicting you, without questioning your motives, your competency or your judgment. Merely the work.

"The work didn't work. Here's what would make it work for me."

"Thank you."

Abbey Ryan, Isaac Asimov and the power of typing

More than a thousand paintings, a painting a day. Abbey Ryan sits down and paints.

More than 400 published books. How did Asimov possibly pull this off?

Asimov woke up every morning, sat in front of his manual typewriter, and typed.

That was his job, to type.

The stories were the bonus that came along for the ride.

He typed when he wasn't inspired. The typing turned into writing and he became inspired.

We don't write because we feel like it.

We feel like it because we write.

You don't need more good ideas, you need more bad ideas

And there it is, as clearly as it can be said.

Instead of saying, "I'm stuck, I can't come up with anything good," it's far more effective to say, "I've finished this, and now I need to make it better." Or possibly, "I finished this, and it can't be made better, but now I'm ready to do the new thing, because look at all I've learned."

This is the story of every single innovation.

This is the story of every good idea, every new project, every pop song, every novel.

There was a bad idea.

And there was a better one.

"How do I make this better?" is different from "How do I make this?"

That's the way our culture works. It's easy to get a committee together to criticize the new logo that your agency put together. It's almost impossible to find someone willing to make the logo itself.

We're a community of critics and tweakers and tinkerers.

The reason is simple: It's safer. People rarely criticize the critic. And beyond that: It's not that hard to use sandpaper. It's a lot more difficult to use a bandsaw, or even a pencil to draw the plans in the first place.

There's a huge clue here about what to do next: Get a pencil.

That's what's scarce. People who will draw up plans. People who will go first. People who ask for sandpaper, now that they've done just about all of the scary bits.

Proving to yourself that creation isn't fatal

"Anchor up" is possible because we have enough experience to know that it won't lead to our destruction. We can only make a sincere promise about the future if we believe we've got a shot at keeping that promise. Ignorance is not a professional's habit.

And so there is the idea of morning pages, or typing up everything that comes to mind, or the, "yes, and" of improv. Each of these tactics is a way of persuading the other half of our brain that we're actually capable of this work on demand.

It doesn't matter if the work is good at first. How can it be? Was Richard Pryor hysterically funny the first time he went to an open mic night? Unlikely. Did Gödel revolutionize mathematics the first time he want to the chalkboard? Of course not.

What these first rounds of public work do is establish to the creator that it's possible.

And then they get to do it again.

Driving to Cleveland—artistic GPS doesn't require turn-by-turn instructions in advance

The magic of GPS is that it somehow knows how to get from anywhere to anywhere else. And it knows how to do it before you even begin your trip.

Think about that.

With the trillions (!) of possible trips, it finds the very best route.

That's nuts.

It's also not the way creativity works. We can't possibly know the route in advance, because so many of the steps involve unknown leaps. We aren't traversing a road we've been down a hundred times before. Instead, we're making our way through the dark, and every once in a while, some light shows up and we have to make a new decision based on where we are now.

Is it any wonder it's so hard to embark on a creative journey of change?

We know we want to get to Cleveland—we know it's been done before—but if we're telling the truth, we really have no idea whatsoever of the best route from here to there. Or at least we won't have certainty after we get started.

News will make you miserable

What if the fear and malaise and anger isn't merely being reported by cable news...

What if it's being caused by cable news?

What if ubiquitous video accompanied by frightening and freaked out talking heads is actually, finally, changing our culture?

Which came first, the news or the news cycle?

We seem to accept the hegemony of bottom-feeding media as some natural outgrowth of the world we live in. In fact, it's more likely an artifact of the post-spectrum cable news complex in which bleeding and leading became business goals.

There's always front page news because there's always a front page.

The world is safer (per capita) than ever before in recorded history. And people are more frightened. The rise of the media matches the rise of our fear.

Cable news isn't shy about stating their goals. The real question is: What's our goal? Every time we hook ourselves up to a device that shocks us into a fear-based posture on a regular basis, we're making a choice about the world and how we experience it.

They want urgency more than importance. What do we want?

If you want to learn to live with uncertainty, the news isn't going to help. It makes us helpless, it pushes us to imagine that we are actors in a play where we have no control over the script. Other than screaming or running away, the news doesn't offer us an out.

But your work demands that you can imagine an out. Your work requires you to embrace uncertainty in service of a bigger, better outcome.

Peers aren't

It would be terrific if you had fellow travelers by your side, the posse that feels what you feel and is as stuck as you are stuck.

But of course, that's unlikely, and it's probably not even desirable.

No one has been in your shoes, no one has felt precisely your kind of stuck.

And worse, if they pretend they have, their feedback is likely to add to your narrative, not undo it.

One more thing: Because innovators are always seeing a different side of things, they're not your target market. It's unlikely that they are the ones who will give you funding or buy your book or donate to your non-profit.

A jury of your peers is hard to find and might not be worth looking for.

Bad grades: The soul-killing metrics of social media

It often takes a special kind of achievement orientation to care enough about the status quo to want to change it.

This is the person who sees something, says something and does something.

This sort of orientation often appreciates feedback.

The feedback of "I noticed this," or, "This mattered to me." And especially, the feedback of "Wow, well done."

Enter social media, with all its numbers and rankings.

This, apparently, is the perfect place to be noticed. An ideal place to measure yourself, not just against previous performance, but against the others.

So you can see how you rank. How you're trending. Who is befriending you (not really—they're not actually friends; that's just a word). Who's unfriending you (a little closer to the truth, or at least it feels this way).

Not only that, but you can read, unfiltered, what they're saying to each other about you. Behind your back and in front of your nose, at the same time.

You can hear not only the criticism and the snide remarks, but most of all, the insecurity your change brings out in other people. You can hear their non-understanding, their jealousy, their fear about the change that might happen next.

Why would you want to?

It's not for them.

Genre is a set of rules; it's the foundation of commercial success—but it isn't necessary all the time

Shawn Coyne has written brilliantly about genre. Not generic, which is boring, but genre, which is a clue, the clue as to what this is about. What's the format? What should it cost? What does it remind me of?

Ski resorts are a genre. So are monster movies.

Without genre, we're unable to process the change you seek to make. It's too difficult to figure out what you are doing and for whom, so we walk away.

But genre has limits.

No one goes out of their way to get a copy.

Copies don't make change.

Genre is a box, a set of boundaries, something the creative person can leverage against.

But then, to make change happen, the artist must bend one of those boundaries, must lever against one of those edges.

How is it different?

Why is it remarkable?

What will I tell my friends?

Ernest Hemingway vs. the novel in your head

I've never met someone who didn't have a good idea somewhere inside.

Do you have one? Maybe more than one?

We all have a plan on how to make work better, or to change an organization we care about, or fix some annoying broken thing in the world. Some of us have a poem, a song or a novel rolling around as well.

What's the difference, then, between you and Gil Scott-Heron? He recorded more than 20 albums and revolutionized an art form. You, I'm guessing, haven't published any.

It's not that Gil's songs are better than yours, or that Hemingway's writing is better than yours. It's that they shipped their work, and you hesitated.

Of course, at first, it's all lousy. At first, the work isn't any good—not for you and not for Hemingway.

But if you're the steam shovel that keeps working at it, bit by bit, you make progress, the work gets done and more people are touched.

There's plenty of time to make it better later. Right now, your job is to make it.

Sam Raimi and the horror of the boos

Raimi is one of the most successful film directors of his generation (*Spiderman*, *Darkman*, *Evil Dead*, etc.).

As a teenager, and later in film school, he insisted on screening his films for a paying audience. "Fifty cents, a dollar, it didn't matter, as long as they paid something."

He discovered early on that paying audiences cared more and demanded more.

Again and again, his work was booed and met with derision.

So he'd go back to the editing room and edit the film. He'd make the scary parts scarier, the funny parts funnier, and then he'd do it again.

Sooner or later, Sam Raimi was making movies.

Which was the hard part? I think it was seeking out the boos.

What happens at meetings (and where did Apple's creativity go?)

The personal computer

The Mac

The iPod

The iPhone

The iPad

And then...?

What happened? Did the culture change? It is the most profitable and valuable company in the history of the world, with years of time on its hands, and it launched a watch. And not a particularly good watch.

Here's an interesting way to look at it: How many totally lame products has Apple launched in the last seven years? Exactly one.

What would have happened if they had found the guts to launch 20 products? A Newton, a Cube, a new kind of software, 30 websites?

As a company grows, the number of meetings grows even faster, eventually reaching a point where so many meetings are taking place that paralysis kicks in.

There are two reasons for this.

The first is simple math. More people needing to be in the loop means more meetings.

But the math clearly doesn't scale, which is why we invented memos and Slack.

No, the real reason is this: Meetings are a great place to hide. Meetings are where we go to wait for someone else to take responsibility. Meetings are a safe haven, a refuge from what might happen.

The poster child for this effect is Apple. As the company has gotten bigger and more valuable, its risk profile has plummeted. Without a driven and sometimes crazy CEO at the top, the company has gotten very good at meetings, but not so good at creative innovation. Their software has stagnated. They cancelled the aggressive date for launching an electric car. Even hardware innovations have slowed, and there's no sign that any of this will change soon.

Steve Ballmer cared too much about being right

Steve Blank points out that Microsoft CEO Steve Ballmer took over Microsoft from Bill Gates and promptly began a multi-year cycle to destroy the company:

> Despite Microsoft's remarkable financial performance, as Microsoft CEO Ballmer failed to understand and execute on the five most important technology trends of the 21ST century: in search—losing to Google; in smartphones—losing to Apple; in mobile operating systems—losing to Google/Apple; in media—losing to Apple/Netflix; and in the cloud—losing to Amazon.

How did he miss so consistently?

Simple: He only did what he thought he was good at. He structured the company to do only things that they were good at. They optimized for the 20TH century and gave away the 21ST century to people who were willing to fail.

Tension is the point

Before we can push an idea uphill (because all useful work is uphill work), we need to recognize that someone isn't going to be happy—and that what we're working on might not work.

Two bits of fear in one action. We're going to offend, and we're going to fail.

But, at the same time, we want the change. We need it to happen. It's worth it.

Hence, tension.

And that tension isn't something to be avoided. It is, in fact, the entire point.

Our ability to dance with the fear and to seek out the discomfort is what makes our contribution scarce and valuable.

Archeologists have less fear than sculptors

Michelangelo famously (but probably apocryphally) described his work as a little like archeology: "Every block of stone has a statue inside it and it is the task of the sculptor to discover it." Sometimes this is paraphrased as, "You just go down to the skin and stop."

Well, if that's all you have to do, let's start. After all, it's simply the gradual removal of everything that isn't the David until—*poof*—you have the David.

But that's not how sculpture (or creativity in general) works. In archeology, there actually is a difference between the dust and the ancient ruin. There's a line between them, there's a correct answer, and diligent and careful work will find it.

On the other hand, there's no line for the sculptor. No right answer for the leader. No correct answer for anyone who seeks to make change.

If Michelangelo had been more truthful but less quotable, he might have said, *"Immagino quello che vorrei mostrarti e poi rimuovo il resto."* ("I imagine what I hope to show you and then I remove the rest.") The hard part isn't removing the rest…the hard part is seeing what you hope to show us.

The uninevitability of your big idea

Big ideas aren't obvious. They bend the history of the future. We don't get to a big idea by slowly scraping off the dirt to find the single obvious truth below.

The big idea, which doesn't happen very often, is indefensible. It's not clear, it's not obvious, and almost everyone who hears it will reject it.

That is precisely what makes it the big idea.

Little ideas are different. Little ideas are good for our ego, of course, because we solved the problem, because we get a round of applause, because we win.

But big ideas, if you choose to seek them out, are unicorns. They are impossible, mythic and almost certainly not attainable.

Which is the point.

Slogans for a new kind of future

No such thing as writer's block

Mise in place is its own reward

Meetings kill innovation

We need more bad ideas

Anchor up and manage the buzzer

Genius is an act, not a person

"If you assume that there is no hope, you guarantee that there will be no hope. If you assume that there is an instinct for freedom, that there are opportunities to change things, then there is a possibility that you can contribute to making a better world..."

NOAM CHOMSKY

PART THREE

Act with intention.

The first question is "Who?" and the second question is "What?"

Now that you've committed to the change you're capable of making, there are two questions that must be asked.

The first question: *Who is this change for?*

And this next step, the next thing you're about to do, *What is it for?*

(Let's call them the Who and the What.)

How will you spend your time and your effort and our resources to make change happen?

That's your new job.

Some people call this strategy

But it's often overlooked.

We often think that we ought to broaden our focus, reach more people and make our offering more accessible.

And more often than that, we build our day based on urgent reaction, not important response. We do things because others tell us to. We follow the pack, guess about what's next and mostly look for small cycles of positive feedback as opposed to digging in deep and thinking hard about what's next.

It's better to call it "design thinking"

Designers create with intention. They understand the power of doing something with an end in mind.

You won't always achieve your end, but your intent comes through in the work, and increases the likelihood that you'll produce the change you seek.

Intent puts you on the hook, of course. You and your team have to own the purpose and outcome of your work, which is why it's tempting to avoid intent and merely do your job.

Please don't do your job. Make a difference instead.

Who is it for?

I'll spot you this: Your wishes are pure, the change is important, it's going to make things better.

And you probably believe that things would be better if everyone got on board.

But everyone won't.

Everyone won't hear you. They won't understand you. And most of all, they won't act.

Eventually, they might come around. Sooner or later, the culture changes. But not because you brought them an idea. Because their friends and family and colleagues do. That's how widespread change always happens.

First from the source, but mostly from the sides.

Who can you reach?

How is it possible for three cowboys to herd a thousand cattle?

Easy. They don't.

They herd 10 cattle, and those cattle influence 50 cattle and those cattle influence the rest.

That's the way every single widespread movement/product/ service has changed the world.

You can't reach everyone.

But you can choose who you'll reach. If you change those people in a remarkable way, they'll tell the others.

And so it begins, "Who is it for?"

Once you choose which subgroup to tell your story to (which subgroup needs to change), this group becomes your focus.

What do they believe?

What do they want?

Who do they trust?

What's their narrative?

What will they tell their friends?

The more concise and focused you are at this stage, the more likely it is that you're actually ready to make change happen.

More and more specific, please

And so the trap. The trap is in the generic. In the cloudy persona, the undetermined person, the vague generality.

Your change is too important to be wasted on most people.

Which people?

Precisely which people?

What do they believe? Who has hurt them, double-crossed them, disappointed them? Who inspires them, makes them jealous? Who do they love, and why?

"Voters" is not specific. "The Lane family, in rural West Virginia" is specific.

Who's it for...

Who is Bob Dylan's next album for? Is it for the person who listened to *Highway 61 Revisited* on the radio in 1968, or is it for the diehard fan who bought the last three albums?

Who is Fashion Week for? Is it for the working woman who is looking for something sharp to wear next week, or is it designed to attract the attention of 100 journalists and trendsetters?

Who is this PowerPoint for? Is it supposed to change the minds of everyone in the meeting? Is it to create a paper trail so that six months from now, my boss will be able to tell everyone that we warned them? Or is it engage the pedants while we spend time having an emotion-based argument with the CEO?

Who is the Hermès Birkin bag for? What about Fox News? Who is donating to the United Way? Room to Read?

It's not for everyone.

Okay, that's obvious.

What about your project, your gig, your organization? Who's it for?

Once we know who it's for, it's easier to accept that we have the ability and responsibility to bring positive change to that person.

Shun the non-believers

If you're marketing a bass guitar or an orchid or an electric SUV, why are you concerned with what everyone thinks about it?

It seems to me that you should only care about the opinion of those that are actually open to buying one.

Someone, not everyone.

Two mindsets

There are two mindsets you can set out to serve when you're asking the "who" question: People who know they have the problem and people who don't.

Solving a problem for people who know they have a problem

A car salesman is going to waste a lot of time selling cars to people who already have a car that runs well, to people who can't afford a car, and to happy pedestrians.

Clearly, people who walk into a car dealership are a lot more likely to believe that they have a problem that a new car can solve.

That's precisely why car dealerships exist. It's more efficient and profitable to let people who need a car come to you, instead of building a business that reaches out and tries to persuade people to buy a car that they don't think they need.

The same is true for just about any change we're trying to sell—it's easier to sell it to someone who begins the conversation by acknowledging that they'd like their problem solved.

Creating a problem for people who don't know they have one yet

This mindset, of course, is a lot more difficult to execute against. It's one thing to sell an SUV to someone in the market for an SUV, but how do you sell the first iPhone, or the first of anything? How do grow a segment and not just take orders?

It begins with this: Realize that this sort of evangelism is expensive, time-consuming and far more difficult than simply offering people a new alternative. And then understand that, in many cases, it's worth the effort.

It's worth the effort because this sort of pioneering work enables you to work with the blue ocean, to define your market, to bring important change to those who can use it but don't realize it yet.

It's worth the effort because you're still tying into something that people already believe. Not that they need the particular solution that you offer, but that there's a desire—for change, for a better life, for connection—that you can offer them.

This person might be curious and interested in what's new.

Or she may be concerned and interested in what will make things better.

Or she may be an engaged member of the tribe, and most of all, wants to stay in sync...

What's it for? The second question...

Once we've established the change, the possibility and the "who," our work begins with a simple question, repeated recursively, until you figure out what's next.

What is this element of our project for?

This is design thinking.

Every element has a purpose. If you don't know what it is, how will you achieve it?

Digging deeper with a simple question

A recursive computer program is one that calls itself. Recursion, the endless process of digging deeper, is an insanely powerful way to simply and effectively get to the truth.

Simon Sinek explored this in his seminal TED talk and book. When we keep asking "why" again and again, we can find our motivation (or realize that we don't have one).

But once you know your "why," you have to do something about it. The challenge of setting our own agenda, the effort of working with others is simple: We need to keep asking what we're doing until we end up doing the right thing.

What engineers know

Everything has a function. Every element of the bridge or the spaceship is there for a reason, even if the reason is decorative.

When NASA engineers put together the payload for an Apollo rocket, there was real clarity about trade-offs.

Everything weighs something, everything takes up space. *Nothing goes on a lunar module unless there's a really good reason.*

The reset

Every time we spend (time, money, trust, attention), we do it in the hope of getting something in return.

Sometimes, all we seek is the satisfaction of having done something well. Or amusing ourselves. Or contributing in some way.

Along the way, we've gotten so good at spending that we do it out of instinct. We spend our time and our money and our trust on things because we always have.

But the world changes, faster every day. What we seek is transformed. The external and internal pressures on us keep changing as well.

There's a simple way to reset.

We can ask, "What's it for?"

In an organization that understands what it's for, the thing we want is the change we seek. Everything we do is designed with that in mind.

That announcement before the flight, when they teach people how to put on their seatbelts…What's it for?

Resumes, job interviews…What are they for?

Working in the office instead of remotely…What's it for?

Spending 30 extra hours looking for typos…What's it for?

Simple example: The receptionist

Every day, hundreds of thousands of people go to work as receptionists.

They sit behind a desk, greet visitors, and do what receptionists have always done.

But what's it for?

After all, with electronic buzzers, cell phones and PBXs, there's really no requirement that a human sit all day at the front desk. Plenty of companies no longer have a receptionist.

Being a pretty good receptionist is easy. You're basically a low-tech security guard in nice clothes. Sit at the desk and make sure that visitors don't steal the furniture or go behind the magic door unescorted.

But what if you wanted to be a *great* receptionist?

If we define the contribution of the receptionist in terms of "what's it for," then becoming a great contributor is straightforward.

I'd start with understanding that in addition to keeping unescorted guests away from the magic door, a receptionist can have a huge impact on the marketing of an organization. If someone is visiting your office, they've come for a reason. To sell something, to buy something, to interview or be interviewed. No matter what, there's some sort of negotiation involved. If the receptionist can change the mindset of the guest, good things happen (or, if it goes poorly, bad things).

Think the job acceptance rate goes up if the first impression is a memorable one? Think the tax auditor might be a little friendlier if her greeting were more cheerful?

So, a great receptionist starts by acting like Vice President, Reception. I'd argue for a small budget to be spent on a bowl of M&Ms or the occasional Heath Bar for a grumpy visitor. If you wanted to be really amazing, how about baking a batch of cookies every few days? I'd ask the entire organization for updates on the day's visitors…"Welcome, Mr. Mitchell. How was your flight in from Tucson?"

Is there a TV in reception? Why not stream some old episodes of *The Three Stooges* or *Prisoner*?

Why do I need to ask where to find the men's room? Perhaps you could have a little sign.

And in the downtime between visitors, what a great chance to surf the web for recent positive news about your company. You could print it out in a little binder that I can read while I'm waiting. Or consider the idea of creating a collage of local organizations your fellow employees have helped with their volunteer work.

One amazing receptionist I met specialized in giving sotto voce commentary on the person you were going to meet. She'd tell you inside dope that would make you feel prepared before you walked in. "Did you know that Don had a new grandchild enter the family last week? She's adorable. Her name is Betty."

In addition to greeting guests, internal marketing can be a focus as well. Every single employee who passes your desk on the way in can learn something about a fellow worker—if you're willing to spend the time to do it, they'll spend the time to read it.

Now that it's clear what the reception job is for, it's significantly easier to do it well. Because like just about everything we do, it's not merely a job. It's for something.

Front to back or back to front

We can begin from the end and work backwards to invent new ways to solve old problems.

Or we can work from where we are and question how we're spending our time and our money to upgrade the solutions we already have.

Begin with the question. This project, this job, this widget, this interaction: What's it for?

And then combine the existence of the resource with the goal we have in mind, the change we seek to make, and the person we seek to change.

Are they linked?

Or, to go backwards, given the change we seek, what have we failed to invest in? What expenditure of effort or skill or resources would contribute an even bigger impact on the change we seek?

The cascade

Consider the apparently simple example of customer service.

In most organizations, the what is simple: For the lowest possible cost, get unhappy customers to stop bothering the company.

If that's what it's for, then by all means, you should have untrained, poorly motivated, barely compensated individuals reading scripts, while on a timer, sharing out-of-date information and, if it saves money, all in a language not aligned with the customer's needs.

This is what most big companies keep track of, manage for and measure.

On the other hand, it's possible for customer service to be part of a cascade in the service of marketing and evangelizing the company's impact.

The math goes like this:

An unhappy customer is an impediment to word of mouth, the key engine of the company's growth.

If we can get the customer to call or email us, we have a chance to transform that unhappiness to delight, and to perhaps do it in a way so remarkable that they tell others.

That word of mouth leads to new trials and purchases.

Which contributes to more growth.

And that increases our ability to change more people into satisfied customers who are reaching their goals.

Well, if that cascade is what you seek, how would you organize and manage the customer service function differently?

It's not that companies are stupid. It's simply that they forgot to ask the question.

Six simple examples of the question

On this expensive bicycle, what's the wheel for?

What's the headline for on this magazine ad?

What's the save button for on this word processor?

What's the airport announcement about security alerts for?

What is the letters to the editor section of the newspaper for?

What is a large front lawn on a suburban McMansion for?

If you think hard about these, you might discover that a lot of what we build or encounter isn't about what we think it is.

In fact, the front wheel of the expensive bicycle exists to remind the purchaser that his money was well spent. This might mean it's loud or exotic looking or fragile...being faster and sturdier is possible, but not likely.

The headline of the magazine ad exists to get the right person to keep reading (and to have the wrong person turn the page). Beyond that, the headline is designed to put the reader into the state of mind where the next paragraph has a chance of getting under the reader's skin.

The airport announcements are for familiarity, not attention. They exist to create a sonic background that makes the airport feel like an airport.

The "letters to the editor" section of the paper is designed to create the illusion that the editors care about what readers think. Particularly the readers who like to write letters to the editor.

The front lawn of a typical suburban house exists as a show of willful waste. The non-productive (and expensive) nature of the lawn itself is the point.

Should a word processor have a "save" button?

If the software's design exists to make the new user feel comfortable, then it ought to work exactly like the software he's used to.

The purpose of the "save" button is to reassure the new user that it's going to be okay around here.

But if the design exists to solve the word processing problems of a committed user, then there shouldn't even be a "save" button.

That's because the purpose of a word processor is to enable people to write. And saving that work is a key element of that. The software is smart enough to save it all by itself. And hard disk space is cheap enough that we can save hundreds of versions, meaning that remembering to save the document is no longer part of what the user has to do.

Going one step further, it's entirely plausible that the "what's it for" of the software design is so generous and thoughtful that users can't help but tell their peers about the software—the design of the software is the marketing of the software.

Which would mean that in every interaction the software has with the user, the what's-it-for is to be breathtakingly smart and remarkably powerful.

Not only that, but it needs to create a sharing dynamic, one that sucks other users in and makes the software work better precisely because it's being shared.

Software like this, then, either exists to be the usual kind and mostly invisible, or it exists to spread the word through delight and connection.

Two different paths, each of which requires the architect of the project to be clear to the team up front about what's supposed to happen here.

Fear

The most common (honest) answer to "What's it for?" is "I'm afraid."

And that's the best reason to ask the question. To discover that while we believe we're working toward a goal, the goal of whatever the work is ostensibly for, what we're actually doing is hiding.

There's nothing wrong with choosing to go to a conference to have fun, or to hide out from work. But if the what's-it-for is to advance your connections and trust within the industry, sitting in the back row and offering no connection to anyone can only be described as a failure.

The what's-it-for recursion lets you choose to go to work, efficiently working toward a goal, whenever you decide it's important enough to ask the question.

What's it for?

We have a meeting at 4 p.m.

Okay, what's it for?

Well, we always have this meeting...

So, the what's-it-for is: It's easier to maintain the status quo than to risk not having the meeting. What the meeting is for is making sure that the people who like having the meeting aren't upset.

Adopting the design-first mindset of intention

Mindfulness is healthy, it's professional and it allows us to be our best self.

It also is maddeningly difficult, particularly in a culture that prizes busyness over just about everything else.

But mindfulness isn't the opposite of busy.

Mindfulness demands intention.

Every moment we spend, we spend forever, and that investment deserves to have a purpose.

What's it for?

We have a new ad campaign.

Fabulous, what's it for?

Well, we have great actors, and a new logo, and wait until you hear the soundtrack.

Sure, that's fun and it looks like a lot of effort went into it, but what's it for?

Our goal is to get more shoppers into stores.

Got it. How does this ad do that?

Toddlers don't get it

Hey, little kid, why are you crying? What's the tantrum for?

He has no idea. He's a toddler.

The hallmark of the unmindful is to react, to lash out, to spend time with no purpose or measure.

When we have no What in mind, we are open to being sidetracked by fear or anger or confusion.

Each of us has worked with intention at least a little. The opportunity is to do it as a practice.

What's it for?

The TSA rule is really clear: You can't put your belt in the same bin as your laptop.

Sure, but what's it for?

It's to make flying safer.

Really? How does keeping my belt out of the bin make flying safer?

Well, it's actually to create a regime of obedience and random anxiety, which makes some people feel safer when they fly.

Oh, got it. In that case, carry on.

Reminder: It's okay to maintain the status quo

Many things we do exist to make those around us feel safe, to help them trust us, to create a foundation for other work.

The answer to the what question might be: "Because we've always done it this way."

And as long as you're pleased with the change you've been getting, doing the same thing to get it again might be precisely the right plan.

What's it for?

We're surveying every one of our customers to ask them 15 things about their buying experience.

Okay, but what's it for?

So we can have a significant body of data about the buying experience.

Oh, what are you going to do with it?

That's not my problem.

But isn't it your job to enhance the customer experience?

Yes.

Then why are you punishing every single customer with a survey we're not going to read?

All the record holders

Isn't it fascinating that in just about every endeavor we keep track of, the world record has been set in the last decade or so? Is this because we're having children who are born with better genes?

Much more likely, it's because the current record sets a standard, a goal, a thing to be changed. Intention leads to focus leads to action leads to results.

What's it for?

I'm going to get a two-year MBA. I just got into Tuck.

Congratulations. What's it for?

So I can get a better job.

Is there a more direct, faster or cheaper way to get on the path you want without spending $300,000 in direct and opportunity costs, not to mention two years away from your career?

No.

Go for it, then.

Working forward

Most of the time, we have a project, we have a system, we have an organization.

But we get stuck in the details.

The details are urgent, the project is merely important.

The details fill us with fear, so we address them first.

We react instead of respond.

We reply instead of initiate.

We embrace the status quo instead of changing it.

"What is it for" is the tool to clear out the details, a practice we can put in place every day.

"I need to check my email right now."

What is it for? Is checking your email actually the next step that leads to the next step that leads to the next step? Or is it merely urgent?

"We need to have a nicer brochure."

Will the nicer brochure do a better job than the existing one? A better job at what? Who will it change? How will it change them?

Could it be that the purpose of the brochure is to assuage our fear and distract us from the important and frightening work of actually engaging with our prospects?

As we go forward, we open one shell after another, working our way through the to-do list, following the trail forward toward our ultimate goal.

Anything that doesn't lead in the right direction isn't worth the detour.

Working backwards

The other method is more challenging. The other method starts from scratch. We begin with the end in mind.

An example:

Our goal is to make a profit. We will make a profit by selling something to wealthy bicyclists.

These consumers want to go fast, to be comfortable and to look good.

There isn't a luxury brand for bike shirts, but there's likely to be an untapped desire for one.

To turn that desire into a demand, we must have an item that's noticeable, covetable, and in some ways, worth paying extra for.

Once we have that item, we must have a retail store to showcase it. And salespeople who fit the image.

That store has to be in a neighborhood that communicates exclusivity and luxury.

And once we have a store, we must advertise it to the right people.

So…When you ask me what this expensive ad in GQ is for, I can answer you. I know what it's for.

Layer after layer

That simple 10-line business plan is only the crudest map for the journey ahead. Over the years, we will layer a thousand other supporting buttresses, a thousand more supportive clues and cues and processes that get us closer to building the change we sought to make.

And every step, we can ask, "Does this get us closer?"

You want to upgrade our fabric? What is it for?

You want to move to a cheaper neighborhood? What is it for?

You want to license our brand to a motorcycle company? What is it for?

Inspiration is overrated

For you, it might be so elusive that it's not worth seeking at all.

Instead, a combination of persistence, focus and guts is all you need.

Change comes from artists. And artists ship. We show up, as professionals, again and again.

We see the world around us, understand genre, but mostly, commit to making a change happen. Not to change everyone, but to change someone.

The best way to do this is with intent. To know what each action is for. To be mindful about our work and its implications.

Of course we're not sure, uncertain about what's worth it, whether or not it will work, and mostly, what right we have to be the agent of change.

Inspiration might be overrated, but the power of our work persists. Our opportunity and our obligation remain: to make things better.

The brilliant director Francis Ford Coppola said, "I don't think there's an artist of any value who doesn't doubt what they're doing."

Doubt is part of the deal. That's when we know we're on to something.

PART FOUR

Questions

"What"

What are you doing that's difficult?

What contribution are you making?

What are you doing that people believe only you can do?

What do people say when they talk about you?

What are you afraid of?

What does the change look like?

What do you stand for?

What is the cost of waiting?

What's the scarce resource?

Would we miss your work if you stopped making it?

"Who"

Who are you connecting?

Who are you trying to change?

Who is ready to listen to you?

Who is willing to be a believer?

What are the beliefs of the people you seek to change?

What are the fears of the people you seek to change?

What are the desires and dreams of the people you seek to change?

What do these people not yet know they need or want?

"Why"

Why is this change important right now?

Why will people spread your word?

What drives you?

Why are you afraid?

Do you believe something is more important than holding onto your fear?

Why have you been waiting?